Dennis O'Bryen, Marq. Charles Cornwallis, John D. Stair

A Defence of the Right Honourable the Earl of Shelburne

from the reproaches of his numerous enemies, in a letter to Sir George Saville, bart. - and intended for the direction of all other Members of Parliament

Dennis O'Bryen, Marq. Charles Cornwallis, John D. Stair

A Defence of the Right Honourable the Earl of Shelburne
from the reproaches of his numerous enemies, in a letter to Sir George Saville, bart.
- and intended for the direction of all other Members of Parliament

ISBN/EAN: 9783337195700

Printed in Europe, USA, Canada, Australia, Japan

Cover: Foto ©ninafisch / pixelio.de

More available books at **www.hansebooks.com**

A DEFENCE

OF THE

RIGHT HONORABLE THE
EARL OF SHELBURNE,

FROM THE
REPROACHES OF HIS NUMEROUS ENEMIES;

In a LETTER To
Sir GEORGE SAVILLE, Bart.

And intended for the Direction of all other Members of Parliament, whose Object is rather to restore the Glory of the British Empire, than administer to the Views of a Faction.

TO WHICH IS ADDED
A POSTSCRIPT
ADDRESSED TO
THE RIGHT HONORABLE
JOHN Earl OF STAIR.

FOURTH EDITION.

LONDON:
Printed for J. STOCKDALE, opposite Burlington House, Piccadilly.
M.DCC LXXXII.

TO

Sir GEORGE SAVILLE, Bart.

SIR,

YOUR country esteems your virtues highly, and she has a claim upon your best efforts. Her condition is distressful beyond all her former calamities. The Earl of Shelburne has taken the lead in her counsels, and the object of this letter is to convince you, that this minister deserves your countenance and support, and the countenance and support of every man like you.

Enmity has done much against the Earl of Shelburne. It is from an apprehension that malice might have some ill effect upon persons even of your character, that I enter upon the task of the noble Lord's vindication: And I have the strongest hopes of proving to your satisfaction, that at this moment of national peril, the man best qualified in this country to direct the cabinet of our Sovereign, is the Earl of Shelburne.

In the broad mafs of human miftakes, not one has blinded the underftanding and deceived the judgments of men more than the common doctrine, which neceffarily unites the gentle virtues of private, with the bolder qualities of public ftation. In plainer terms, that a bad man cannot be a good minifter. The fpecies of argument I am about to urge will not perhaps be popular. It works againft the fpirit of vulgar morals without doubt. But, Sir, I write to oppofe and not to indulge the miftaken prejudices of the world, that world which is at once the knave and coward of the creation, perpetually playing every fallacy, and blindfolding itfelf with difguife and affectation, confcious of truths, which it has not the courage to inculcate.

The virtues of little life are, without queftion, a vere fine fubject for declamation. It is eafy to be eloquent upon the arts that foften the pains that heal up the wounds of human beings, and the deeds that exalt, ennoble, and confer a fort of divinity upon, our mortal condition. But, I do affert, that the rigid honor which laughs at law, and looks with contempt upon all artificial conftraint, the faith which binds men together by the facred force of truth, and the candor, which fcorns all deception,

ception, are qualities, however admirable and excellent in the sphere of narrow life, not only unneceſſary to a miniſter, but that theſe virtues really impede and thwart him in political purſuits. I enter a caveat againſt all haſty judgments, and deſire to be tried fairly, and patiently.

But although the *reality* of virtue is not only needleſs but abſolutely a dead weight upon a miniſter, truth muſt confeſs with Machiavel and Bolingbroke, that the *appearance* is not always injurious—it is ſometimes expedient, but never indiſpenſable—without even the appearance, I do maintain that a miniſter may acquire power, and for a long time preſerve that power.

Providence has happily deſtined men for different walks of life. It is not every man that is fitted for a court, nor have all men an equal right to great ſpheres and ſituations. *Non omnia omnibus cupiunda.* There *may* be a foil for inflexible honor and rectitude of mind, but a court differs from every other ſcene of life, and in no particular more than in this, that vices ſeem to loſe their own nature, aſſume the ſhape and produce the beſt fruits of abſolute virtues. The thing would puzzle us in theory, if daily facts

facts did not demonstrate, that the same man can be at once the *King's friend*, and an enemy to all the King's earthly interests. How many men have acquired opulence, and maintained power in this country, upon this very principle, for the last twenty years!

A man that has talents, or thinks he has, should seek a scene of action by any means. What are abilities without the opportunity of exertion? Power is the medium, and every method to obtain power is sanctioned by the motive. *Neque facto ullo, neque dicto abstinere, quod modo ambitiosum foret.* Ambition (says a great poet) is the glorious fault of angels and of gods. Is there a reasonable man who can condemn Alberoni for the arts he practised, with a view to future greatness? Alberoni was even a pimp to the monstrous pleasures of the Duke de Vendome. Vendome placed Alberoni in that sphere whence he grew up into a prime minister of Spain, and in the very *means* of his exaltation, the man gave an earnest of the talents which in a few years afterwards blazed upon the world from the minister.—Instances of this sort are out of number.

Since society has been polished into the establishment of a court, how few have ever acquired political influence, or, acquiring, retained that in-

influence, by the auxiliary of bare virtue! The principle of my reasoning is not weakened, because two or three solitary cafes, like exceptions to a general rule, may be pointed out. A minister should rise to power by any expedient, and, risen, he should retain it at all hazards. No axiom is more simple or more certain.

How seldom have states received any extraordinary benefit from the extraordinary virtue of public men; but the evils are written legibly upon the records of most countries. Cato's improvident honesty burst asunder the only union that could have saved the Roman republic, if the salvation of the republic had really been (which I sincerely doubt) an advantage to the Roman people. Oppose the conduct of Cæsar to Cato. Cato stigmatized the people with avarice, meanness, luxury, debauchery, extravagance, and injustice. Cæsar praised the people for every public and private virtue. His deportment was humble and complacent; his actions gentle and generous. Will any man say, that Cato was fit to lead a government? Could a great people endure to be insulted by the very person who sought their support? And when I see Burke at Bristol, with his bundle of virtues upon his back, daring to claim, not indemnity, but honor, for the very deeds
urged

urged against him, as crimes, I lose my patience until I see his presumption, the folly of which is enveloped in its audacity, punished as so gross an outrage deserves. The events at Bristol and Utica should be considered as eternal monuments of the wisdom and spirit of Englishmen and Romans!

But, Sir, to come more directly to the subject in contemplation—The minister who hopes to prosper would adapt his mind, his habit, and his practice, to his peculiar situation. To poets and philosophers he would leave the beauties of theoretic virtue. He would humble himself to the plain imperfect condition of mankind, and govern himself accordingly. He would have craft for candour, subtilty for solidity, and fluctuation for firmness. He would abandon integrity for expediency, and confirm that cunning was more beneficial than capacity. For open and decisive measures, he would have a silent system of dark and impenetrable operations; no matter how despicable, so it be obscure. As Ægyptian priests concealed the frauds of their religion, so should a minister hide the weakness of his projects, under the mask of mystery. He would have all the show of personal attachment, over the most fixed contempt for genuine friendship. A minister would declare

clare and deny the declaration, affert and revoke the affertion. He would now feem completely decided upon a meafure, which the next day he fhould reprobate, as never entering into his head. He would have a temper to accommodate every kind of inconfiftency. Above all other artifices, a minifter would excel at intrigue. Intrigue is a magical veftment, which would afford him a cloak in all his tranfitions, variations, and windings; if like a Proteus, he affumed all fhapes, natural and unnatural. A minifter would ftop fhort at no impediment to obtain his object, though he break through all the barriers of private friendfhip and public confiftency. He would ftudy the leading weaknefs, and predominant attachments of the Sovereign, and adminifter moft devoutly to his wifhes, either as the pimp of his loofe paffions, (according to the inclination of the prince) or the pander to his political principles, however miftaken or fatal. He would reprefent the popularity of a rival, as treafon againft the ftate, and the diffatisfaction of the people againft himfelf, as a difaffection to the Monarch. He would do whatever elevated and ftrengthened his own power, and neglect *nothing* that tended to degrade or injure his enemies and opponents.

A judicious minister must be always suspicious of eminent genius, or extraordinary merit, in others. It is remarkable, that in a few months after the great Conde vanquished the foes of the King of France, Mazarin (the minister of that King) confined Conde in the castle of Vincennes. Turenne conquered all before him, and Louvois (the minister) was constantly undermining Turenne in the favour of that King, whose glory Turenne had been increasing by daily victories. Does any reasonable man censure Mazarin or Louvois? It is the commonest of maxims with a minister, that the interest of the state is ever to yield to his personal resentments. Lewis the Fourteenth, when he invaded Holland, wished to keep garrisons in all the Dutch towns. Conde and Turenne were strongly against the measure; but Louvois seconded the King, because he hated Conde and Turenne. The garrisons were continued, and this mistake preserved the Republic of Holland from annihilation. Mazarin and Louvois were great ministers.

Perfection is not the gift of God to man.—And if this sketch be not the exact resemblance of the Earl of Shelburne, I will venture to say, that the noble Lord comes as nearly to the spirit, as human frailty will allow.

allow.—The friends of Mr. Fox, the rival of the noble Lord, imagine that *he* might be, at least, as powerful a minister as the Earl of Shelburne, from the advantage of his superior talents. But this is the dear mistake of mankind—Superior talents are no security for superior success in courts, where trick is as beneficial as genius, and cunning is frequently more prosperous than capacity. Let us for a moment view the honorable Gentleman and the noble Lord in the lesser relations of life, and from the contemplation of the two men, let us decide which seems best calculated to succeed in the cabinet of our Sovereign.

Both have been bred in all the forms of fashionable life, but Mr. Fox appears to be satiated, and is grown into a contempt for all external decoration. The laborious levities of a late peer are objects only of his ridicule. Perhaps he esteems the ease and politeness inseparable from a man in the habits of high society, as sufficient, without resorting to any artificial means of creating notice, or impressing regard. It is not unreasonable to assert, that if pomp of dress, prettiness of manners, or exterior neatness constituted much of a man's real dignity, a valet or hair-dresser would stand a better chance than John de Witt, or the Earl of Chatham. This seems to be Mr. Fox's opinion. He puts on a fine dress sometimes from duty, but never from inclination.—The Earl of Shelburne cannot deem a shining coat in itself a thing of any consequence, but he thinks it is an instrument by which the multitude may pay their homage of amaze. I have heard him apologize to the House of Lords for '*presuming to come undressed*;' and I dare say without any implication of censure upon twenty other noble peers, who needed purification as much as himself, at the same moment. He has the substantial precepts of the Earl of Chesterfield * for ever in his eye, and seldom neglects the essential article of a splendid outside.

Mr. Fox seems so averse to the subtilties of life, that he rather deters by distance, than seduces by familiarity.—Every syllable uttered by the Earl of Shelburne, every gesture of his body, and every motion of his face, are accompanied with a design either to invite the indifferent, to conciliate the hostile, or to flatter the friendly, by an indefatigable assiduity, by a politeness that perseveres, and a smile that never ceases.

* Les Graces.

The creed of Mr. Fox is, to prefer candor to complaisance, and rough frankness, to polished falshood. If he makes an engagement he thinks he should not violate his faith. He imagines, that the ties which bind the private, constrain the public man. Under this disadvantage he went into government, making few promises, and breaking none.—The Earl of Shelburne has not a heart to refuse a request, and it is difficult to impeach him with an infallible breach of promise, inasmuch as no man can limit the measure of life. If he does not perform, who can assert that he *may* not. A thing is morally possible, where it is not physically impossible. While there is life there is hope, and to despair of happiness is impiety. The noble Earl, with great management, separates the private from the public man, and with a curious refinement and dextrous discrimination, acquits the Earl of Shelburne of any treachery or meanness, which may be committed by the First Lord of the Treasury.

Mr. Fox has a respect for the judgment of the nation, but looks to the purity of his actions for public applause. He never accommodates himself to the devices which very often influence the general voice, and indolently endures a present evil, in confidence that his genius and integrity will rectify all in the end. —The Earl of Shelburne is convinced, that ministers have heretofore been powerful and perpetual, in spite of the people's clamours, and has the most settled contempt for the world's opinion. But he knows its value, and if his system of small arts fail him, he may sometimes relax into rectitude to acquire or preserve it.

Mr. Fox is careless, where the Earl is cautious, and candid, where the Earl is cunning. His friends love him, although he is seldom at the pains to please by study. When he was opulent he never dreaded indigence; he is not wealthy, and yet despises riches. He will sit with the man he values upon the simplest fare, as contented as at the feast of a king.—The Earl of Shelburne is the eternal slave of his society. He courts every man. His placidness, his attention, his humilities are endless. He has the craft to appear a public enemy to luxury, and yet yields to none in the vice he censures. Penurious by nature, and extravagant by system. He has the skill to make his selfishness assume the form of generosity, and to make real sordidness resemble hospitality. He condemns

demns the spirit of the democratic body, but thinks the grandeur of the aristocracy impaired, if domestic pomp and outward magnificence are in the least neglected.

If a man is ridiculous, Mr. Fox will laugh at him; and if he is a rascal, he is very apt to tell him so.—The Earl of Shelburne never hurts a man in his presence, but delivers himself with a generous indignation against those who are absent.

Mr. Fox thinks himself right, and virulently reprobates those he thinks wrong. He is no apostate, and gives little quarter to those who are. —The Earl of Shelburne never offends the ear of the greatest knave upon earth with a harsh epithet: he knows that severity of reproach may create desperation, and therefore never irritates. —Mr. Fox has in this respect so little artifice, that he would censure an obnoxious measure, even to the Sovereign who employed him, with a harshness for which the sincerity of his counsel could hardly compensate, and which perhaps rendered his advice something more than barely unpalatable.—The Earl of Shelburne has been so industrious, even before he became a minister, that he never omitted to offer some incense,

when-

whenever the King's name was introduced in debate. He knew the temper of his deity, and seldom failed to sacrifice.

Mr. Fox is an utter stranger to all facility, and never softens out of complaisance into another's opinion. From the day he burst the bandages of his political childhood to this hour, he has pursued one invariable line, without the smallest deviation. His system is defined and decisive.—The Earl of Shelburne is above the weakness of persisting in a principle which militates with his interest. He is not rash enough to adhere to any series of opinions which may impair his power, although his honor and consistency were the victims of his compliance. He never entertains a peevish prejudice for old sentiments when they are inconvenient, and has so fortunate a ductility, that he can bend to all sides, and adapt himself to all situations. He has been twenty years an actor upon the state theatre without any fixed character. His politics are so judiciously ambiguous, that no man can ascertain their quality, from which results this good effect, that he is absolutely, *nothing*, and may be occasionally, *any thing*. He is in profession a Whig, and a Tory in practice. He pretends a regard for the people's rights,

rights, and is the unqualified champion for prerogative in its moſt wide and dangerous operation.

The ſympathy which kindred qualities naturally excite, attaches Mr. Fox to men of letters, but he never ſought their flattery, and his patronage was never very beneficial. He is no ſycophant, and abhors thoſe who are. His own vanities are enveloped in his ambition, and he never adminiſters to the weakneſs of another. —The Earl of Shelburne has a vaſt diſplay of patronage, but the talents of moſt of his clients *were* of ſo abſtracted a ſort, that out of the eight millions who inhabit this iſland, not eight perſons will ever take the trouble to judge of their merit. The praiſe he applies in a higher, is acceptable to himſelf in a leſſer ſphere, and no man pays at a dearer rate for panegyric [*]. His aim is to be ſpoken of, and he would compound for eclat by any ſacrifice.

The noble Lord, as well as the honorable Gentleman, is ſuccefsful in diſcovering the imbecilities of the man he converſes with; but they are very different in deducing conſequences from

[*] The daily papers ſhew that the noble Lord's patronage is lately much extended.

the

the infirmities they detect. What Mr. Fox's pride difdains to ftoop to, the Earl of Shelburne's œconomy endeavours to fhape into the poffibility of fome immediate or future benefit. The latter deems that valuable, which the former looks upon with contempt. The whole ftretch of the Earl of Shelburne's abilities exceeds not the compafs of what is termed *intrigue*. Mr. Fox defpifes intrigue. He confiders it the talent of a fool and a rogue. He thinks no man but a knave would make much ufe of it, and no man but a blockhead would boaft of it.

Such is Mr. Fox, and fuch the Earl of Shelburne, upon the leffer fcale of life. To thofe who know them beft I appeal for the fidelity of the pictures. The abilities of the noble Earl will come under frequent difcuffion in the courfe of this letter; but you will obferve, that I have excluded the talents of Mr. Fox entirely from our confideration. To analife him in a view where his public enemies to a man fhrink from beholding him, would not become me. All parties are long agreed in that point, and perhaps the thing moft undifputed, in this land of difputes, is the genius of Mr. Fox. Enough however is feen of his principles and temper, to fhew the delufion of his

his friends in imagining that *he* was calculated to prosper in an equal degree with the Earl of Shelburne, in the court of George the Third.

TO SUCCEED where there is no impediment, is a puny merit. The dexterity of a statesman is manifest in proportion to the magnitude of his difficulties. If a minister is surrounded with danger, perplexed by inconsistency, and involved in a labyrinth of doubt, to emancipate himself with *safety*, is a trial of his management, if not of his talents. A good deal in this situation stands the Earl of Shelburne. Parliamentary support is very justly deemed the test of political truth in this country, and I hope my confidence is not too sanguine, that the noble Earl's measures will be supported in the next sessions of parliament.

In the Upper House at least he cannot fail, and it is a comfort to a minister of England, whoever he be, that if, like another Caligula, he had made war upon the moon, that illustrious and reverend body is sure to give its sanction to the planetary adventurer.

There are four or five points which are supposed particularly to affect the Earl of Shelburne, and he is said to be especially vulnerable as to the American question.

Petitions

Petitions have been presented by some of the people against the American war, and the Parliament voted its discontinuance. Hence it is said, the people of this country are averse from the measure of its revival. Upon this occasion (however at other times it may be expedient) I believe the noble Lord would not insist upon that general maxim of all British ministers, that the wisdom and wishes of the nation reside in the Parliament; or indeed, if he were disposed to make a concession in argument which operates against himself in fact, I, who write to defend him upon the principle of truth, would not therefore concur in the opinion. I deny the proposition and the inference, and have no dread in asserting, that it is *not* the wish of the majority of the English nation to abandon the American war.

The lust of dominion is natural in every soil, and the love of superiority is as prevalent in this land of freedom, as in any part of the earth. The English love to be masters, and he is at least a crafty minister, who takes advantage of their prejudice. The people is his sanction, and his ignorance or treachery is sure of being sheltered under their delusion. The English love to hear of bloody battles, and a snug citizen in the corner of a coffee-house, who

who would shrink at a snow-ball from the hands of a boy, deems the Gazette he peruses, a libel upon his country, if half a thousand of his fellow-subjects have not perished in the engagement, let victory incline as it may.

The opinion of Lord North is decidedly with me upon this question, and I trust Lord North's opinion is still highly valued in this country. "I have had the majority of the people with me in the American war," said his Lordship. He said the truth, and the people's voice is still the voice of God. It is true, that a six years ineffectual struggle, at a great waste of blood, and an expence of one hundred millions, afford but an inauspicious review upon a revival of this war; yet who is the man daring enough to step into the chair of fate, and pronounce the *impossibility* of success, if we make *one more* bold and brilliant effort? Such a man is not to be found; and I am well convinced, that there is not an individual in the nation with British generosity, British courage, or British feelings, who would not contribute '*even his last shirt*' to regain those colonies, of which we knew not the importance, or extent, until their intire loss gave a mortifying evidence. Reports of a disaffection to congress in some of the colonies already prevail, and it is surely a species of suicide

suicide not to have an army to co-operate with those who are still attached to us. We have already, upon various occasions, felt the good effects of our American friends, and there is not a doubt, that by vigorous efforts, in two or three more campaigns, some of the continental provinces may be strongly inclined to negotiate with our commissioners. It is worth the experiment at all hazards.

But the accusation against the Earl of Shelburne upon this point is two-fold. He is charged with duplicity to the Parliament, and treachery to his friends, in having first implied an assent to American independence, upon the formation of the new ministry, and having afterwards reprobated that measure as destructive of all the interests of this country. This charge I admit up to the full point of conviction, and hence deduce all that is necessary to establish my original position, that the Earl of Shelburne was destined to be the minister of George the Third.

The King naturally loved the object of the American war, however as a man he may be shocked at the horrors incidental to military operation. A new ministry must be formed, and those who overturned the old system must in grace and decency be, or appear to be, at the head of the new fyftem. The Earl of Shelburne is his Majefty's meffenger to invite his former friends, and Lord Rockingham, Mr. Fox, &c. are leaders in a plan of government, one of the chief objects of which is to grant American independence. The noble Lord has the darknefs to hide his real defigns, as to this great principle in the new adminiftration (it is no matter to us whether in compliance with any contract in the royal clofet, or from other motives) and forms a miniftry which he is convinced muft burft to pieces in a few months. Let me appeal to your judgment upon this occafion, and afk you, if, upon the face even of this tranfaction, the Earl of Shelburne does not appear to be a man fit to profper in a court? It is no anfwer, that any man may be a knave, and that the bafeft blockhead may deceive the brighteft genius. There is a train of management and myftery throughout this bufinefs, to which neither envy nor enmity can refufe applaufe.

Treachery to his friends! a minifter laughs at the exploded term. It is a language which exifts only to be defpifed. The Earl of Shelburne has the example of one of his prefent colleagues before him, that no tie fhould bind

bind a statesman; and the less temptation to infidelity the greater virtue in the villainy. I scarcely need remark to you that I mean the Duke of Grafton. He who grew into power under the patronage of Lord Chatham, and deserted him the next day. He who cordially united with Lord Rockingham, and abandoned him immediately after. He who by turns sought the favour, and equally abused the confidence of Lord Bute and the Duke of Bedford. He who made Lord North a chancellor of the the Exchequer, and after plunging him into disasters, left him to shift for himself,—even as he betrayed his Sovereign, in the most distracted hour of his reign. If sympathy of soul can arise from similitude of nature, the Duke of Grafton and Lord Shelburne must be connected. Both have given a thousand proofs that they can never differ but in the degrees of deception. Principle cannot separate them, and if in the variety of ministerial virtues which mark the character of the Duke of Grafton, any one part could, more effectually than another, link himself and the Earl of Shelburne close together, it is certainly this—that the Duke, in the affair of Corsica with Choiseul, made the Earl of Shelburne the most contemptible dupe that ever signed a King's dispatch as a secretary of state.

And

And it is said the noble Lord can never concur in American independence, without covering himself with disgrace, as he has publicly pronounced that minister a traitor who assented to such a measure. This kind of argument seems specious, but it is really false. A minister's consistency is always accidental. The noble Lord has already begun to soften down the rough parts of this political dogma, and upon the last day of the last session of parliament, he did, with a curious sort of finesse, refine it, in saying, that he thought ' the sun of England was set that day England should grant independence to America.' The recess has been employed in melting and meliorating the implicitness of this opinion still more, and if he should be forced indeed to recognize the independence of his Majesty's American dominions, I have not a doubt the noble Earl, when he signs this death warrant of the British empire, will come off in a very courtly and minister-like manner.

The noble Earl is supposed to rest upon this alternative. If he abandons the American war he disappoints the King; if he renews it, he deceives the nation. Granting this to be exactly the case, a minister who is determined to retain his situation, may surely steer a middle way,

way, and avoid the two dangers. He is said (from a terror of rivals out of the cabinet, and to indulge some strange spirits in the cabinet) to have offered independence to America by Mr. Grenville and Sir Guy Carleton, and that America has refused it. America does not fight without an object. Her object is to be independent of the British crown, and it is ridiculous to think she would not accept what she has been seven years shedding her blood to obtain, if it were offered her in an unquestionable, undeceptive form. I could suspect the noble Lord's cunning to have tendered independence in *such* a shape, as infallibly secured its rejection; and I could suspect his making this refusal the instrument of a parliamentary sanction to renew the war. These are conjectures, and time must decide. Perhaps the noble Lord has no such view. He may not in this point impose upon either the people or the prince. He may neither renew the war, nor yet grant independence. He may let the affairs of America vibrate through another indecisive year, and prolong his ministry, by keeping alive the public solicitude. Wealth is valuable, and power is precious. Who but an ideot would resign while he could retain? There may be such a thing as executing the *King's business* in a hurry, and closing the sessions without any

final

final determination. Precedents may be found in abundance. The Earl of Shelburne knows the materials of the English. They are a fusceptive people. It is a nation of confidence, and a fine promise has a proud effect. The good sense of the people may be convinced, that it is material to the national honour not to decide upon the American question *yet*. Philip the Second growled for three years, before he acknowledged the independence of Holland. The noble Lord has this wise example before him. We have gaped a long time for events, yet time brings about wonders. The principle of our patience is still alive, and surely those who trusted Lord North for seven years, cannot refuse one year to the Earl of Shelburne.

The second charge against the noble Lord is, that he intends to spread the mantle of ministerial impunity over the East India delinquents.—This sort of accusation lessens the necessity for long defence. The measure carries its own vindication along with it. The Earl of Shelburne has not a heart to be cruel; and is there any cruelty more palpable than to strip a man of the fruits of his industry? The noble Lord's lenity in this case will not only be charitable, but it will be politic. Could any thing be more unwise than to discourage men from scenes where opulence accompanies victory, and the love of glory is not the *entire* impulse to action *?

At a season when public prostitution has weakened the vigor of the human character, and private luxury has blunted the edge of military ardor, a stimulus *must* be left to animate men into adventures. It is reasonable, and other countries have felt its benefits. Without question we shall hear it said, that the Lord Advocate of Scotland, who so nobly begun the career of oriental reformation, cannot, without incurring disgrace, relax in his efforts to correct the depredations which are a stain in the national character, which render the name of Britain execrable in every region of Indostan, and which the learned Lord himself has often solemnly pronounced to deserve punishment, as necessary to the salvation of all our interests in the East. But an anodyne taken in the nepenthe of St. James's might work a wonderful oblivion, and I am greatly mistaken in the disposition of Mr. Dundas, if the present treasurer of the navy cannot easily persuade the Lord Advocate of Scotland, to forget all the rapine and barbarities he heard of in the butcherly neighbourhood of Leadenhall-street.

* Sese quisque præda locupletem fore, victorem domum rediturum.

I mean

I mean, if the Earl of Shelburne deem it necessary, and I sincerely trust his compassion and policy will not be deterred by those bellowers for justice to the Indians, in the House of Commons. Men of wisdom and virtue, it seems, are going out to assure the natives of Asia, that we have an earnest mind to be honest, and rob them no longer. All memory of bills of penalties must be washed away, and I hope to see Sir Thomas Rumbold, one of these days, baked up in a batch of Irish peers, and Mess. Whitehill and Perring, joint plenipotentiaries with Mess. Vaughan and Oswald, in securing the dignity of the British empire, and restoring Europe to her former harmony.

A third reproach upon the Earl of Shelburne is, that he will advise the King, to revive his negative to disagreeable acts of parliament, *if the people insist upon a change in the representation.* And will any man deny that the King has the right, however weak people may discourage the exertion of the right, at the very moment it is probable the Parliament may speak the sense of the nation? The constitution would not have placed a privilege in his hand for a mere mockery. Great writers have indeed asserted, that a King of England may be the most absolute prince in Europe by the noblest means, those of reigning in the hearts of his people. But what is the dictum of theory to the conviction of experiment? The interests of King and people must be separate, or wherefore all the treasons, rebellions, civil wars, oppression, violence, and butcheries that have distracted the world these three thousand years? The whole tenor of his present Majesty's reign demonstrates the fact. The laws invested the King with the negative; no part of the prerogative is more defined, and if he leaves one of his best privileges much longer in a state of inaction, a stubborn people may be induced by and by, to dispute its constitutional authority, from the antiquity of its operation.

The Earl of Shelburne is supposed to have immersed himself, in declaring that "he would never listen to the sound of a King in Ireland." Perhaps the noble Lord has great reliance upon the Irish parliament. Experience justifies a confidence in that assembly, which has appeared to the world more than once, within the last two years, to yield in virtue and spirit to no senate of Greece, Rome, or Britain in their purest days, but superior to each, with a defined object, and animated by the first of motives, yet before the close of each sessions, to be the most servile.

vile, base, and profligate mob, that ever met to betray the rights, and juggle the understanding of a nation.

Lawyers affirm that precedent presumes repetition. It is possible a similar temper of ductility may be still found in the Irish parliament; and it is probable the noble Lord depends upon the senate of that country to secure him from another inconsistency. But it needs no mighty labour to prove, that the Irish parliament has, more than once, received hints from the Irish people. A nation (even without the forms of freedom) may sometimes feel that political abuse is carried too far. The sentiment still better becomes a nation who have at least the semblance of liberty. The Irish people felt it, and the parliament felt the people. There are qualities in the British constitution which rise above the grossest corruption, and the people sometimes speak a language which must be understood. It is evident that the principles of the Irish volunteers, as well as of their friends in the senate, is, if not in shape, unquestionably in substance, diametrically opposite to the Earl of Shelburne. Yet I dare not doubt, if the tide of Irish politics run against him, that the noble Lord will be completely insensible to embarassment, in advising the King of England to receive that

that petulant coxcomb the King of Ireland, with all possible courtesy, and not feel himself at the same moment, the less a great minister.

Mr. Fox is said to be popular, and the Earl of Shelburne execrated in Ireland. It is not my maxim to run a muck at truth, and tilt at facts. I believe the fact is exactly so. Mr. Fox, upon opening the Irish business, did certainly desire, while he officially delivered the decision of the cabinet, not to be mistaken, as one brought into that resolution by a majority of the administration, but on the contrary to be understood, both in England and Ireland, as giving the naked sentiments of his heart (at the same time that he opened the intentions of the King's council) from the conviction of long thinking and mature reflection. He said the Irish sought no more than '*substantial justice*,' and upon Lord Beauchamp's recommending, as well a repeal of the principle of the 6th of George the First, as of the act itself; Mr. Fox heartily concurred in the noble Lord's suggestion, if he thought that mode would be most pleasing to the Irish, adding, that the method adopted was not that which he deemed the best, but it was the method demanded by the Irish themselves, and he thought an exact compliance with their wishes was the most gracious way, in which

their

their rights fhould be acknowledged by the Englifh Parliament. Mr. Courtney, from well-meant but miftaken pride, confidered the fuggeftion of Lord Beauchamp, rather as tending to fanction the ufurped claim of England, than as neceffary to emancipate or fecure the liberties of Ireland.

Much comment has been made upon Mr. Fox's diftinction between internal and external legiflation, and I believe he has not been well underftood upon that point, on either fide of the channel. His remarks feemed to me to have had no other object, than a cenfure of the old adminiftration, whofe oppreffive conduct fo irritated the people, that in fhaking off the internal legiflation of a foreign parliament, they equally reprobated all ideas of the external, which, in the hands of an honeft miniftry, they would probably never complain of as an evil; but the folly and injuftice of the old government had made them impatient until every reftraint was taken off*. The remark was a fort of digreffion, in which not a fyllable implied the leaft defire to retain any affumption of power over Ireland, in the Englifh Parliament. What fell from Mr. Pitt, who feconded the

---

* This fubject will be more clear to thofe who know the nature of the *Irifh free trade*, and *Irifh fugar bills*.

motion,

motion, was both untimely and unjuft, and muft have furprized Mr. Fox, as well as moft others who heard him.

Thefe circumftances, united with the tenor of his political conduct for eight years, and the predilection which fome perfonal knowledge is apt to create, render Mr. Fox a favourite in Ireland. The Earl of Shelburne opened the Irifh bufinefs in the Houfe of Lords upon the fame day; but in a manner lefs handfome, lefs liberal, and infinitely lefs acceptable (according to general opinion) in his native country. Certainly his conduct upon that occafion tended only in a very fmall meafure to diminifh the prejudices of the Irifh againft his Lordfhip.

Sir, the Earl of Shelburne lives to illuftrate vulgar apopthegms more than any other man breathing. It is fome comfort to be fortified by the moral of old fayings—No man is a prophet in his country, fays the proverb; and I will venture to affirm, that his warmeft advocate (if indeed he has one more ardent than the writer of this letter) will not deny, that the Earl of Shelburne has been long difliked in the kingdom of Ireland. That his countrymen deal unjuftly by his Lordfhip there is no doubt, and I will mention one circumftance to prove

that

that they do. It is a trifling anecdote, and as well known in Paris and Vienna, as in Dublin or London.

The founder of the Earl of Shelburne's family was Mr. William Petty, a surgeon by profession, and a man of unquestioned merit in science. Mr. Petty was appointed to survey the kingdom of Ireland, after that kingdom begun to breathe from civil diffention. In executing this commission, it is supposed the surveyor forgot to insert in his muster-roll some portions of land, which he transmitted afterwards to his own family, and which his posterity inherit at this day. The lands were uncultivated, and of course of no value. A greater accession of property was acquired to the family in another way.

When Cromwell ravaged the kingdom of Ireland, he had no money to pay his troops, and, instead of cash, conferred by patent upon each soldier a certain portion of ground, the birthright of many of the antient nobles of the nation. Cromwell's soldiers resembled Cromwell. He loved to live upon the best kind of animal food, they had no stomach for vegetable diet, and could never digest potatoes. The lands were sold in consequence, and a butcher might become a baron, if he had money. The buyers had mighty bargains. I have seen a tract of beautiful ground, containing eighty acres, which was bought for two English crowns. Of all the purchasers of these patents Mr. Petty was the most considerable; the extent of lands which he transmitted to his family was immense; and, such is the transition of human affairs, that the old proprietors became tenants to the new purchasers. These lands were derived from the family of the Pettys, by leases of three lives, renewable for ever, upon the tenants paying half a year's rent on the fall of each life. In progress of years a great many tenants had, either from neglect, or the remissness (voluntary or otherwise who can decide) of the agent to the estates of the Earl of Shelburne, suffered some of the leases to expire, without paying the fine of half a year's rent. The late Earl of Shelburne brought ejectments against the tenants upon this omission, the tenants filed bills against the Earl of Shelburne, and obtained injunctions to stay proceedings at law. The matter was suspended in court, ' when the act of God deprived' * the tenants of the virtues and the talents of their noble landlord. The late Earl went to heaven, and the present Earl went to Kerry. The son was too

---

* Part of Lord Shelburne's speech upon the death of Lord Rockingham.

pious

pious to neglect his father's example. He carried on the suit with vigour, and during its progress in Chancery convened a great number of his tenants, and offered them leases of thirty-one years, without any written covenant of renewal, but engaging solemnly, upon the sacred honor of a peer, if those tenants who rejected the proposal, and trusted to the law, did legally oblige him to give better terms, those very terms to the minutest part should be granted, *bona fide*, to the tenants who accepted the proposal. The offer was irresistible. A preclusion from law expence, with all the possible benefits of law, the Earl of Shelburne, young, and then unmarked by any infamy, which made it very improper to place a confidence in his solemn voluntary vow. Several of the tenants acceded in consequence.

The Irish Chancery some time after, upon an equitable composition as to the fines, decided in favour of the tenants, and the Earl of Shelburne was compelled to renew, according to the letter of the original leases. Those who accepted his Lordship's proposal, demanded the advantages of their fellow-tenants, conformably to the spirit of their compact with the noble Lord.

I do not find it in the bond, said his Lordship,

* Shylock in the Merchant of Venice.

The Earl of Shelburne knew of no written article of legal compulsion, and absolutely refused to renew: the tenants went home, crying, 'we have not acted like wise men!'

Why should the noble Lord renew the leases upon the obligation of a verbal contract? he may read the statute-book up to the last volume and find no penalty incurred, no express law violated—nothing to censure him—nothing to coerce. It would have been idiotical, if, from any crawsickness of conscience, or honor, he had renewed. The lands under the old leases do not produce a sixth part of the current value of similar estates in Ireland. Who could be mad enough to mind a promise to men with such names as *Mlaghling o'Muynighane—Philimy Mackcullacotho—Moroogha mac Lughullugha?*——Or who could dread that such men, creeping through life in a neglected corner of the most distant county of Ireland, would ever come forward with any impotent efforts, to fix a stain upon the unsullied probity of the Earl of Shelburne?

* This is a trifling incident, and I record it only to shew you, that the same principle of

---

* The writer of this letter undertakes to *prove* any man who should contradict the preceding anecdote *a liar.*

deep

deep management, and provident sagacity, which inspirits the public conduct of the Earl of Shelburne, accompanies him through the lesser concerns of private life; and as one proof among the many thousands already in the public knowledge, that the noble Lord was perfectly right in declaring (when he did intimate to the House of Lords the King's intention of his succeeding the Marquis of Rockingham at the head of the treasury) that ' for his Majesty's favour his intire reliance was upon *his own integrity.*'

When the Duke de Sully came to his inheritance, he found the family estate of Rosny in the most deplorable condition, and his tenants the most wretched in all France. By humanity and industry he made the estate in a few years the most fertile and elegant, his tenants the most contented and comfortable in the whole kingdom. A friend asked him, upon his becoming minister to Henry the Fourth, whether he meant to manage France and Frenchmen as he did the estate and tenants of Rosny? The Duke's reply was, that his practice as a minister should be precisely upon the same principle that he was a landlord. He kept his word to the minutest part. France was the most feeble and wretched kingdom in Europe upon the Duke de Sully's accession to power,

—he

—he made her the moſt flouriſhing and formidable monarchy of Chriſtendom. The Earl of Shelburne found his tenants in eaſe and happineſs. He left them in indigence and miſery. No man can ſuſpect that I would by this draw any preſumptive inference againſt the noble Lord's adminiſtration. His recorded virtues would render me as ridiculous as my argument would be unreaſonable, if I attempted it.

You, Sir, are an Iriſh landlord, and as your treatment of your tenants has been exactly upon the plan of the Duke de Sully, I am inclined to think an adoption of the Earl of Shelburne for a model, might greatly improve your treaſury;—but I have ſome fears that his example will not eaſily tempt you to heap calamities upon your tenants in Ireland, even though the product of ſo infamous an avarice (inſtead of making you the baſeſt fellow in the nation) ſhould only continue to honour you with the title of being one of the beſt gentlemen in Britain.

For the above reaſon, and for reaſons ſimilar, the Earl of Shelburne is obnoxious in Ireland. In that quarter he has certainly great impediments to encounter. But if the Iriſh Commons, upon whom he has, and upon whom I have,

have, great dependence, should not answer his purpose, the Lords, who indulged him with annihilating the revenue officers bill, cannot fail. A congenial temper of commodious facility prevails between the peers of Ireland, and their noble brethren of England. Never were two assemblies more capable. But if it were possible, that most virtuous and venerable body should deviate into a forgetfulness of their old flexibility, the noble Lord is not destitute of other sources of support in that country. The rights of the Irish nation have been often enveloped in the splendor of the Irish court, and whatever influence the acknowledged genius of Lord Temple will fall short of creating, may be supplied by Lady Temple's well-drest Mercuries. If the Earl of Shelburne's efforts to seduce Mr. Flood, in his late visit to London, have been ineffectual (which by the way I do not answer for, tho' it is not probable he has been successful) the noble Lord has a just confidence in the Earl of Nugent's * popularity. The Earl of Nugent is almost as great a favourite in Ireland, as the Earl of Shelburne; and, I have no doubt, both the one and the other would be as well received in that kingdom, as Velasques was in Portugal, or Verres would have

---

* Lady Temple's virtuous father.

been,

been, if he returned to Sicily. The measure of the Irish fencibles was a bold attempt, but unhappily too palpable. I fear that will no more succeed than the scheme of ships from the English counties. It is a great misfortune to this administration, that the Irish people of late have felt *themselves*, and the greatest evil of all is, that they seem to know the Earl of Shelburne completely.

SENECA speaks of somebody who wrote a treatise upon the benefits a man may receive from his enemies. The writer alluded to by the philosopher, should have been a politician. It is the criterion of a minister to make use of his foes as well as his friends; and the noble Earl, whose cause I am endeavouring to vindicate, yields to no mortal in the full practice of this best of maxims. From his foes (the Northites) he got a principle, and from his friends (whom I shall call Foxites) he got a theatre to put this principle into action. The Foxites overturned the Northites, and the Earl of Shelburne became a minister in consequence. He had a sort of Ottoman virtue, and could bear no brother near the throne. He would be a Turk—nay, he would be a Christian to get power. He made it impossible for the Foxites to remain in the cabinet, and sent them to erect a fortress

for

for the reception of General Conway, when the General, in his turn, should be a fugitive from Paradise, unless indeed he wish to languish between the elements, like a fallen angel in Pandemonium.

How far the noble Lord has got a principle from his foes, hear the assertions of Mr. Fox, uncontradicted by two of his colleagues, at that moment present *: ' there are things that ope-
' rate upon a man's belief, which are not demon-
' strable. I cannot absolutely prove to this house,
' what I am in my own mind convinced of—
' that the Earl of Shelburne has views inimical
' to this country; but this I will say, that if
' the late secretary at war had sat in the King's
' council, he could not more assiduously have in-
' culcated that system of unconstitutional prin-
' ciples which we have been so many years en-
' deavouring to overthrow.' Doubts are best decided by analogy, and the people of England will not be extremely puzzled for Mr. Fox's meaning, when he assimilates the Earl of Shelburne with Mr. Charles Jenkinson.

Sir, if I could be persuaded that this imputation of Mr. Fox affected the Earl of Shelburne, I might argue like a lawyer, and say

* On the 9th of July in the House of Commons.

that a bare affertion comes far wide of proof, and confequently of conviction. But I fhould be a lawyer indeed to quibble, where common fenfe is more effectual. It is upon this very fyftem of political thinking, which Mr. Fox fo loudly reprobates, that I build the chief defence of the noble Lord.

Idem per alterum is true wifdom—How can I tell, or how can you tell, by what variation of manner the fame end may be purfued, or by what dexterity of minifterial difguife the GREAT ORIGINAL OBJECT may be concealed from the vulgar eye. That object which begun with Lord Bute—which the Duke of Bedford adopted as the only channel of grace—which Lord Chatham and Lord Rockingham difdained to countenance —which the Duke of Grafton afpired to eftablifh—which he delivered to Lord North—which Lord North was forced to abandon—which the Earl of Shelburne grafps to his bofom, and will, if poffible, depofit in its long expected fanctuary. The fhape may be changed, but I have no doubt of the fimilitude of fubftance. Thofe who are moft friendly, and thofe who are but lukewarm, to the noble Lord, have ftrong fufpicions. His opponents to a man are decided. Therefore I have faid that the Northites gave him a principle.

That

That the Foxites gave him a scene, is a position which admits no question. The noble lord thought his dignity somewhat diminished by continual parliamentary exertion, and imagined that the seldomer he appeared, he was like another Bolingbroke*, 'gazed at like a comet.' Upon the Duke of Richmond he left the burthen of opposition, and never did man more faithfully or more firmly persist in political projects than the noble Duke. The Duke of Richmond debates as a Swiss mountaineer fights for his liberty. He hits an adversary with every weapon; nor is it a flash, nor a figure, nor a flourish, that can dispossess him. I have seen the noble Duke lose even his legs in argument, and like another Witherington he has battled the enemy upon his stumps, until prelates, and lay peers, and law peers were forced to seek an ungallant victory in the coup de main of a division.

Upon this noble person rested chiefly the exposition of the old system in the House of Lords. The Earl of Shelburne indeed came down upon nice occasions, with a well-dressed speech. The species of eloquence called *reply*, seems not to be much admired by the noble

---

* Henry the Fourth.

Lord. Reply subjects most speakers to slip into inadvertencies. The Earl of Shelburne seldom repeated his speech in the House, without discovering that sort of *design*, which I think fits him for his present station best of any other man.

For instance, he came down upon the first day of the last sessions to shed a patrician tear upon the calamity of Lord Cornwallis, and whilst he reprobated the ministry for carrying on the American war, pronounced a florid panegyric upon the King for implying a desire to pursue the very war he affected to execrate.—Observe this fact, Sir, and tho' you may deny candor to the senator, the praise of cunning at least is due to the statesman.

The Earl of Shelburne likewise came down upon the attack on the French convoy in December by Admiral Kempenfelt, not so much to abuse the Admiralty for ignorance of the size of the French fleet, as to convey a proud idea of his own information from the continent of Europe.

The noble Earl also came down upon the affair of Mr. Isaac Haynes—and whilst Lord Huntingdon attacked the Duke of Richmond, on the one side, with the loveliest assemblage of features that ever softened the rigor of an enemy, and the Lord Chancellor surrounded him, upon the other side, with Grotius and Puffendorff, and Cocceius; the Earl of Shelburne afforded his noble friend the Duke no other assistance, than pronouncing an eulogium upon the greatness of Lord Huntingdon's ancestry (an information perfectly new to every man above and below the bar) and directing a most fastidious frown at Lord Stormont, with these important words—" upon this day, the 4th of February, no system of conduct appears to be formed by these great men." Lord Stormont is any man's match at a stare of emptiness. He looked back upon the noble Earl like a gilded calf. The Earl of Shelburne continued almost in the words of the poet, ' A nation's fate depends on you'——' Cockadoodle do,' replied Lord Stormont, with an erectness of eye-brow, and loftiness of forehead, which would not have disgraced the elder Vestris, when he receives the crown from the hands of Creon.

Through these, and through all the parliamentary operations of the Earl of Shelburne, you must trace a *plan*. Success constitutes the merit of all actions, and his must therefore be called

called a judicious plan. He looked for the hour, it was flow, but it was not the lefs certain. Kings *are* the beſt judges what quality of ſtateſmen are moſt ſuitable to their cabinets. It is petulant in Monteſquieu to ſay, ' That after all he cannot help having ſome pity for ſovereigns, who are generally ſurrounded from the cradle to the grave, with knaves and ſycophants.' It is eaſy to be eloquent, and men in their cloſets may rail at the inſidious policy and treacherous arts of ſtateſmen, but inſidious policy and treacherous arts are neceſſary to a government!

The Earl of Shelburne is a man who muſt proſper in a court. He knows when to relax, and when to tighten the line. Look at his conduct upon the late volunteer bill; ' You ought to have power to force the people,' ſaid Lord Stormont—' I admit your principle,' replied the Earl of Shelburne; ' Government, for true political uſes, *ſhould* have a power of compelling the ſubject. Your maxim is excellent; but we muſt reſort to gentler methods. The policy would be better to adopt bolder means, but this is not the ſeaſon.' And if you will enquire the particulars of the progreſs of this bill, I believe you will find, that

the

the Earl of Shelburne admitted the greater part of Lord Stormont's amendments, and recognized *all* his principles of government.—Perhaps Sir Charles Turner would cry out, *Alius et idem.*

This neceſſarily leads me into a ſhort conſideration of another part of this noble Lord's character. It may ſeem ſtrange to ſay, that the man who is deſtitute of political conſiſtency, ſhould be endued with political courage. Yet I think the noble Lord in his own perſon abſolutely reconciles this apparent paradox. I do believe he has ſome ſhare of boldneſs. It is to this Mr. Burke alluded, when he affirmed in the Houſe of Commons, that he thought it twenty times more dangerous to truſt the Earl of Shelburne with power, than the old miniſtry; whilſt Lord Mahon kept writhing at Mr. Burke, like a gladiator. ' Will you lift this Marius, ſaid Mr. Burke, over the Metelli, over all the good and honeſt men in England? Will you put power into the hands of Sylla?' Yes certainly, I would ſay (were I a member of that houſe) I would truſt power into the hands of Lord Shelburne, who does I muſt confeſs reſemble Sylla. *Ad ſimulanda negotia altitudo ingenii incredibilis, multarum rerum*
et

et maxime pecuniæ largitor, is Salluft's portrait; and yet I would truft power with the noble Lord—Befides thinking with Mr. Burke, that the littlenefs of manners, and mediocrity of character, which are the types of the prefent generation, forbad exactly the effects of the confidence in Sylla—I know it is extremely poffible that the Earl of Shelburne may not turn this power into a fatal ufe. I know it was poffible when power was conferred upon Sylla, that he might not deluge Rome with the blood of her beft citizens. It is faid, that Sylla had a ftrong mind *not* to enter upon the bloody bufinefs of the profcriptions. If he did not deem it neceffary to his own confequence and fafety, he would probably not have murdered thofe heaps of Romans that make their hiftory horrible.—In that refpect the firft law of nature was his fanction.—But furely it is ftretching apprehenfion too far, entirely to compare the men, and the fituations—our own pure unfanguinary fcaffolds do not at all countenance thefe fine apprehenfions.

This country, I maintain it, wants a bold minifter. Could its hiftory have been fullied with the violences of June 80, had this noble Lord been at the head of affairs? How did the Earl of Shel-

Shelburne act upon that occasion?—Sir, with the discernment of a man fitted by nature and art to be a minister, he declared, '*he did not doubt, but government itself was at the bottom of the riot;*' and he stated an instance to illustrate his conjecture.

He naturally concluded the riot could never have grown into such an alarming magnitude, unless it had the countenance of administration. Had that noble Lord been minister, no judge would have been obliged to torture statutes, or hang fifteen ragamuffins upon a single indictment. Sir, there was a mode of suppression more obvious—a punishment more convenient—Not a good citizen will hesitate to confess, that, to vindicate the national order, ten thousand men should have fallen, as the victims of that violence; and I am forward to assert, that the inertness of the army upon that occasion will be an eternal stain upon the free government of this country.

The Earl of Shelburne was justified in suspecting that administration. To discredit a minister is proverbial. There are times and circumstances which forbad a confidence in any man. *Ne Catoni quidem credendum.* I will not trust even Mr. Fox upon this occasion, said Sir

G   George

George Saville. I must have an explicit assurance concerning the American war. But whether the administration of the year 80 were guilty, or not, these conclusions are fair.—First, that their imbecility upon the affair of the riots will be a blot upon our annals.—Secondly, that extraordinary powers should be placed in the hands of a minister, and that the minister be a bold one. The Earl of Shelburne will, I trust, prove himself a bold minister. My only concern is, that our niggard constitution has shamefully constrained the authorities of his office; but I have much reliance upon the Parliament.

Without enduing the Parliament with the attribute of omnipotence, in imitation of Sir William Blackstone, it is yet certainly competent to remedy that fatal defect in our civil form, which very often binds up the hands of a minister, and only leaves him the mortification of speculating in private, what he dares not publicly execute. Does any man doubt the temper of the Senate? Is any man mad enough to imagine, that the temporary triumphs, the partial victories of last March, have entirely annihilated the great *principle* of Parliament— the great principle of human nature? Corruption can only die of a supernatural death. The success of those, who, in the last winter, barbarously

barously checked the spring that gives energy and animation to political movements in this country did certainly astonish the world; yet their victory was dearly bought, and no miracle accompanied their glory. The stamina are yet in a state of wholeness. They only wait a little cultivation to vegetate in full fecundity, and bloom out again in their antient vigour and mellowness. Human nature is not very subject to extraordinary conversions, and Jugurtha and Sir Robert Walpole will still maintain their station among moral philosophers. *Omnia mortales pecunia aggrediantur.*—Men may think, and stammer, and stutter, and doubt, but they will decide after all, and they will decide with the ruling passion. *Vicit in avido ingenio pravum consilium.*

Was the great and shining feature of Parliament impaired or altered upon the motion relative to Mr. Rigby last June? So far from it, that the house, which for two months before exhibited a solitary aspect of depopulated benches, could scarcely contain the crowd of senators, who came accoutred with wry faces, 'like Herod's hang-dogs in old tapestry,' to give a home thrust to that impious missionary, who threatened ruin to their antient tenets, and meditated the destruction of their old religion.

—Per-

—Perhaps a final thrust—The report of a dissolution was then current. It is probable the administration of that day imagined the nation would not be the worse if a certain class of senators returned to their counting-houses, and mansion-seats near the capital. But I will venture to affirm that the Earl of Shelburne has no such design. The genius of the present parliament is well known. Characters more capable are not easily found. Much address is necessary to seduce a virgin — the strumpet yields to every libertine that pays for her prostitution. The Earl of Shelburne is convinced, it is not every good man in the Lower House, who can twice in two years afford the sum of four thousand pounds for a seat in parliament, especially when contractors bills, &c. do apparently preclude him from serving his country in the way most suitable to his own wishes. From *you* at least I shall not hear, ' that the parliament will not dare to betray the interest of the nation,' I have your own words publicly delivered in the senate, how far it is possible for a parliament to go to the very excess of political infamy. In the year 1770 you asserted, ' *that the majority of the House of Commons were traitors*'—and when I am convinced that the present parliament have given so many proofs of superior consistency, wisdom,

wisdom, and virtue, that their integrity should not be questioned, it will be a greater happiness to me to place a confidence in their honesty, than to live in a persuasion that they can equal the profligacy of any of their predecessors.

The bills passed last sessions, for excluding certain members, and for restraining certain ministers, are supposed by some good people to defeat the possibility of corruption. It cannot be denied that these bills render political seduction a more difficult task. But where is the man of truth, and plain sense, who shall affirm that corruption is impracticable? Some of the bills are worded with all imaginable caution, and it must be admitted, that a First Lord of the Treasury cannot, with very great amplitude, practise the old trade of parliamentary corruption, without committing a perjury. But surely even this is a trifling impediment in the great career of so aspiring a minister as the Earl of Shelburne—a political oath at the Treasury should be as much a matter of form as a commercial oath at the Custom-house; ' *a politician has always two consciences.*' There are ingenious modes of evading any law. It is the glory of English judges (tho' a great foreign writer has reproached them with it as a crime) to attend to the *letter*, and consider the *intent*

of

of an act of parliament as a secondary object. Can a minister have any example more august, any sanction more venerable, than the unspotted practice of British judges? And surely no statesman can be such a botch at logical distinctions, as not to find a convenient position to entrench himself behind the *letter*, whilst the *spirit* of a law might waste away, like the spirit of Plato in his visionary republic.

From an expedient management of the parliaments, the Earl of Shelburne will, I trust, obtain, not only a great enlargement of power, but a sanction for stretches of power, when necessary. Weak men suppose that the Lower House cannot, through any temptation whatever, support his administration, inasmuch as the noble Lord has been at all times wantonly forward to disparage the democratic branch of the constitution; and even in the last sessions, has taunted that body with the epithets of ' a petty aristocracy, a septennial nobility,' &c.—When the Earl of Shelburne affects the *proper* feelings of the House of Commons, I have not a doubt they will shew a very *natural* spirit. A point of avarice could not fail to create a contest, but I cannot suspect them of so improvident a revenge as quarrelling with a First Lord of the Treasury, upon a mere question of ambition.

And

And this is the golden hour of opportunity for a great minister to perpetrate great designs. Facility in general accompanies felicity, and no man can say that the English do not seem to be a happy people. There was a cowardly sense of danger in the Roman republic, which we disdain to feel. They had confidence, it is true, in the midst of distress, but they were the most shamefully apprehensive people in the world. The historian tells you, that Rome shook to her center, upon the loss of a battle, even in Africa. *Metus atque meror civitatem invasere, pars dolere pro gloria imperii, pars timere libertati, omnes tristitia invasit, festinare, trepidare, afflictare sese, omnia pavere, superbia atque deliciis omissis.* You observe, Sir, that they feared even foreign calamity had endangered their domestic liberty, and considered their fame and freedom as blended together.

But with *us*—there is a noble negligence, a sort of generous contempt, and illustrious indifference to public measures and incidents, that tho' three thousand veteran troops were captured, three million of subjects lost to the crown, and thirteen colonies dismembered from the empire, all is frolic, and mirth, and gaiety—The commerce of perfumes at least does not slacken; nor is the elegant and liberal art of a

French

French dancer the less sure of the distinguishing patronage of the English gentry. (These remarks are vulgar, but who can dispute them?) Pluto and Epicurus seem our only deities. Review the opera-house upon the ruin of Cornwallis—you would imagine the temple of Janus had been shut up, and that Mars was only engaged in cuckolding Vulcan: while the British theatre was perhaps entirely deserted, and Shakespeare and Congreve abandoned for Simonet and Metastasio.

Our glory is, that what others have done from expediency, we do from election. Lewis the Fourteenth blinded the city of Paris with tournaments and festivities, at the very time his own and Madam Maintenon's jewels were sold by public auction at Amsterdam.—His gaiety was artful, ours is entirely natural. Royal personages are very active in our pastimes likewise, but whom I sincerely acquit of having Lewis the Fourteenth for a model, or of being impelled by any political motive under heaven.

Such, or nearly such, was Rome in the days of Sylla *—completely such in the days of

* Urbem venalem, et mature perituram, si emptorem invenerit.

Cæsar.

Cæsar. Such was Thebes, and such was Athens in the time of Philip. That Athens, where the bare sound of appropriating to the calamities of the state, a small part of the stock-purse for public amusements, created an absolute rebellion.

The subject, Sir, upon which I address you, contains much matter, and a vast complexity of argument. It imperceptibly leads to digression. I fear that all I have said is not apposite to the plan of defending Lord Shelburne; but I have not deviated wantonly, and shall be more in order for the remainder of this letter.

THE ANTAGONISTS of the Earl of Shelburne will no doubt arrogate an infinite merit to themselves, for having acted towards the people precisely as they engaged to act. Great promises lessen credit, said Mr. Burke. *Multa fidem promissa levant.* They have a right to say—we gave justice to Ireland, and she gave us in return an unusual gratitude*, an accession of strength equal to ten ships of the line.— Had our advice been accepted an open and honourable conduct should have been held towards

---

* If Ireland is not satisfied, her discontent is not chargeable upon the Rockingham administration. They recognized her rights exactly *in the way she prescribed.*

America.

America. How far we were right in the policy to be adopted with her, look to the effect of the negotiations at Paris, to the rejection of all overtures from Sir Guy Carleton, and the refusal of a passport for Philadelphia to his secretary—We should have acted to all the dependencies of the empire with equity and liberality. The only mode of regaining the confidence of our fellow-subjects in the different parts of the world, is to treat them as the citizens of a free state, and not as the slaves of tyranny. *Melius visum amicos quam servos querere, tutiusque rati volentibus, quam coactis imperitare.*—We gave the nation a contractors bill, a revenue-officers bill, a civil list bill *.—Out of office, we reprobated the corruption of parliament; in office we exhibited a spectacle, new in the history of our country. *The minister of the day* (Mr. Fox) *decrying the influence of the crown, and supporting the power of the people upon the treasury bench*—We went into government with pure hearts, we left it with pure hands.—These are the methods by which we give the lie to those who called it unconstitutional in Mr. Fox to appear upon a Hustings in open day, to recommend a man of tried probity to the free choice of his constituents. If they were in-

---

* I will venture to say, that nine out of ten of the revilers of this bill never read it.

deed enemies to Mr. Fox who traduced him upon this occasion, and said, 'How would *he* have bellowed had Lord North appeared upon a hustings?'—it serves only to prove an old position, that a foolish foe, is a real friend. I think Mr. Fox hardly needs to have better advocates than such revilers. Their political conduct leaves no doubt of *their* regard for the constitution. The tenor of their whole lives puts it out of all question.

Lord North upon a hustings!—He, who for twelve years supported the most pernicious system of government that ever marked the fate of any unhappy country, not excepting any period of the most rapid decline of the Roman empire. He who, in seven years, dismembered the most powerful state of the modern world, by the most universal system of corruption that dishonours the history of Britain. Sir Robert Walpole, in the infamous glory of his most extended turpitude, yields as much to Lord North, as the wealth of the state, in the time of the former, exceeded the riches of government under the latter minister. Was there one question of public policy decided in either House, during his administration, but by the palpable influence of positive bribery? Was there a county or city election, in which he did not interfere? Was there a contemptible borough in the whole kingdom which he did not purchase, or endeavour to purchase? Is it any satisfaction that he was not *in person* upon the various theatres of corruption? Lord North's body is unweildy, but a First Lord of the Treasury has mystical faculties. His influence is omnipresent. How did he act in the very county of which he is Lord Lieutenant? His faithful Commons (for no partial distribution of a loan had then made them faithless) acquitted him, it is true, of having directly interfered. But I appeal to the understanding of the public. Was there in this nation one man of honour and good sense, who did not in his conscience believe that Maurice Lloyd went to Milbourne Port, to undermine the interest of Temple Luttrell by the desire of Lord North? I say, *was* there? Because the matter has been since put out of all question.

That only one acknowledged minion should be returned at the general election, was as necessary to the public credit of Lord North, as it was requisite to the private purse of Mr. Medlicott that he should (when all was quiet) accept the Chiltern hundreds. But the train of measures, by which Mr. Luttrell's petition miscarried, was base and infamous beyond all conception.

ception. I do not impeach the committee. Perhaps they decided up to the spirit of their oaths. The shameful arts practised to defeat the petitioner were probably out of their knowledge, but they should be recorded for public information, and parliamentary example. The most shameful advantage was taken of the distresses of an unfortunate gentleman, and the people at large will be shocked to hear that a witness [*], amply sufficient to overthrow the opponents of Mr. Luttrell, was secreted in a house at Lambeth, until the petition was decided, and afterwards recompensed with a generosity that far exceeded the abilities of Mr. Medlicott, and not at all disgraceful to the munificence of the treasury.

That the class of politicians, who have made it a merit in Lord North, not to appear upon a hustings, should traduce Mr. Fox for doing so, is a circumstance which I will take upon me to say, *he* will never lament. Such enmities never fail to be useful. But whilst Englishmen have hearts, and hands to execute the wishes of their hearts, a minister like Lord North will not dare to appear upon a hustings in the city of Westminster. And if Mr. Fox

---

[*] This creature's name is *Hyde*.

(who

(who has overturned that abominable fyftem of univerfal corruption, the political Hercules who deftroyed the political Hydra) fhould ever tread in the footfteps of Lord North, as a minifter of this country, I wifh, when he appears at a place of election, he may meet a fate as much worfe than the death of Raviliac, as the affaffin of a good king, is a more innocent character, than the murderer of a glorious conftitution.

The antagonifts of the Earl of Shelburne will afk, What has the noble Lord done for the people? Nothing—but he has promifed every thing. 'Thefe bills (fays Mr. Fox) are pigmies to his promifes, but they are giants to his performances.' They will urge further, can the Earl of Shelburne fhew his face, convicted as he ftands of flagrant falfehood, as to Mr. Fox's refignation, by the according voices of Mr. Burke, Mr. Fox, General Conway, Lord John Cavendifh, Lord Keppel, the Duke of Richmond, and indeed by his own confeffion. How can that minifter retain his ftation, who has not the confidence of any part of his Majefty's dominions, who is accufed by all his enemies, and whom no friend dares to vindicate. On the 9th of July he was ftigmatized in the Houfe of Commons, as as a minister without merit or genius, as a man without truth or fidelity, and not a soul rose to speak in his behalf, but one impotent individual, at the close of the debate, whose defence was damnation. To those I have but one answer. So long as he maintains his present situation, just so long I allow him merit. The minister who promised every thing, and performed nothing—who overturned his friends, and increased his own power at the same moment, is in my opinion the true genius of minister. You may say, it is treachery, and rail at cunning. You may quote Bacon and Bolingbroke against it, say it is left-handed—it is the low mimic of wisdom—it defeats itself in the end, and so on: yet, Sir, I affirm, it is the great and superior talent for a minister of these times.

The noble Earl is fond of cant terms. I will give him one which has been popular in the nation ever since the 9th of last July. It is called a day *famous for his infamy*. The minister of England reprobated, in the House of Parliament, with all that can degrade a man and a politician, without a defender, without a friend. And yet who is it can positively say that there may not be, after all this, in the world (though not in Kerry or Wiltshire) some

some person who *can* speak well of the Earl of Shelburne? A bad character should not be the ruin of a minister. Mazarin was the idol of the court, at the time he was detested all over France, and obliged to quit the kingdom. I think in principle he resembles the Earl of Shelburne,—for similarity of fortune, I affect no prophecy. If the Earl of Shelburne is hated, the people is giddy, and I do not despair to see a plenty of panegyrists start up even in the House of Commons this next sessions. The noble Lord, as Mr. Lee remarked, is in the way of making friends—and will not, I am sure, misapply the patronage of the treasury upon this score. His friends too will have one great advantage over the panegyrists of Lord North. A lover's tongue never faulters so much, as before the object of his adoration. I have seen the blooming Mr. St. John languish down even while he cast the thurible, with the smoaking incense; and many a time, when the gracious divinity was snuffing up the perfume, has the priest fainted under the weight of the sacrifice. The Earl of Shelburne's friends, unawed by his presence in the Lower House, will have none of these embarrassments to encounter. Flattery succeeds best in fiction (according to Waller, who was certainly a judge) and I hope to hear many a splendid

splendid eulogium upon the Earl of Shelburne, this winter in the House of Commons.

With some people Colonel Barré is accusable for his silence upon the 9th of July; but I can well acquit him—To *him* at least it was a trying hour, and it was natural the patron should be absorbed in the pension. I have got these three thousand two hundred pounds a year, for twenty years laborious duty in parliament, said Colonel Barré. That's wrong, replies the Earl of Shelburne, the next day in the House of Peers. The Colonel gets this pension, because all the good *I* have already done, and all the blessings I shall yet bring upon this nation derive from him. I am in the way of a Messiah, and ' OWE ALL TO HIM THAT SENT ME.'——My conduct, says the Colonel again, upon General Warrants in the House deprived me of my rank in the army, my government and military emoluments. This pension is given me as a compensation.—Wrong, replies the Earl of Shelburne: He get this pension as a bargain for Mr. Burke's getting the paymastership. Lord Rockingham was the proposer of it—That's a flat falshood, cries Mr. Burke (who has sometimes a downright plain mode of talking) I appeal to Lord John Cavendish.— The matter originated with Lord Shelburne, fays Lord John. I never heard of its being in lieu of the paymafterfhip.—The noble Earl talked of this penfion, cries Mr. Fox, before the miniftry was abfolutely formed.—This and all he has faid yefterday concerning my refignation, are no more nor lefs than direct and palpable deviations from truth, and I fhall prove them fo.

The fact is fimply this—Colonel Barré derived neither his government nor military emoluments originally from length of fervice, nor eminence of merit in the army. He owed them, exactly as he does his penfion, to his conduct in the Houfe of Commons, when his friends were in adminiftration. He oppofed a fucceeding miniftry, and loft his places. I am not going to juftify his removal, but every man knows, this very policy has been the general practice of moft adminiftrations in this country. And if the Colonel's claim to a penfion were really examined and then admitted, two hundred men might ftart up to-morrow with equal rights, upon the fame principle. A few arguments of this fort would have greatly puzzled the Colonel.

I agree with you, Mr. Barré, ' that honour has its delicacies.' You fpoke emphatically. ' I vow

vow to God, if there is one honeſt ſenſible man in this houſe, who would ſay that I did not deſerve this penſion, I would never take a ſhilling of it.' Truth is one of the lovelieſt qualities of honour. And I aſk you as a man of honour, do you believe there was one honeſt ſenſible man in that Houſe (thoſe who concurred in the meaſure excepted) who in his conſcience thought you deſerved that penſion, ſituated as you then were, and circumſtanced as this unhappy country is at this time? If you ſay *Yes*, I ſay *No*. I do affirm that it was not the wiſh of that Houſe, nor is it of the nation, that you ſhould get a penſion, whilſt they who had ſuperior claims, and ſuperior neceſſities, never received, nor ever ſought (to their honour be it ſpoken) a ſingle pound. There is no ground for cenſure upon the feceding party as to this: a proviſion for an old friend (however they may ſilently diſapprove the meaſure) was too ungracious a cauſe for conteſt. But the fact is, that the power of this country was in the hands of the Earl of Shelburne, and every incident ſince the moment he ſaw the King laſt March, to this hour, confirms it. Mr. Coke it ſeems heartily regrets not dividing the houſe. 'Had he done ſo, Colonel Barré would have had as much occaſion as Mr. Dyſon, in days of yore, to ſing the Lamentations of Jeremy the prophet; but fortunately for him the magic monosyllable decided his fortune.

The Colonel however is a grateful man. He retired twice with Mr. Pitt, and I thought his countenance told me, as he returned by the Speaker's chair, that the recruit muſt be ſent to drill. At length the Atlas of the hour *did* ſtart up, but not a ſyllable fell from him in defence of the Earl of Shelburne. On the contrary he ſunk the noble Lord deeper in the mire than all his enemies. Would Cato have taken Cataline for his colleague, ſaid Mr. Pitt (admitting the implication in its full force) —Yes, replied Mr. Burke, " A good man, for a great end, will ſuffer the leſs to avoid the greater evil. Cato *might* have taken Cataline for his colleague, as Cicero abſolutely united with Antony, there are ſeaſons of public peril when the greateſt oppoſites muſt be reconciled for the public ſafety. The Earl of Shelburne was the meſſenger to us from his Majeſty, and we admitted him, not from choice but neceſſity."

It is ſaid, that Mr. Pitt (whoſe merit ſeems to conſiſt much more in a ſelection of elegant
lan-

language, and a placid style of elocution, than in any great vigour of imagination, or sagacity of intellect) will probably administer but little consequence to the Earl of Shelburne's administration. Mr. Pitt proscribed himself from all inferior stations, and proclaimed his disqualification for the objects of his ambition. It was a task fitted for the earl of Shelburne to reconcile the scruple and gratify the vanity at the same time. The most extended knowledge in the mere theory of politics is supposed to be not half so necessary to a chancellor of the exchequer, as a thorough acquaintance with the interior of a kingdom, and with all its resources. Study, unaccompanied by great experience, can hardly confer these advantages. But the difficulties of the office enhance the flattery to the officer. Mr. Pitt perhaps was irritated by the loss of his brother's bill, and yet no common offer could seduce him. But this was a temptation which must have braced the shattered sinews of old age, and very naturally melted the green fortitude of aspiring youth. His rank in all the future administrations of which he may be a part, was defined at once. The glory of transcending even his father was not to be resisted. He held not the reins of nature, and could not, like Joshua, lengthen out the day. Such another

other hour could never occur. A chancellor of the exchequer at twenty-four was brilliant beyond the vulgar records of civil dignity. There is a splendid boldness in great attempts which excites our wonder, and we excuse the folly of Phaeton, in the magnitude of his ambition.

To passion therefore, and not to principle, are his admirers willing to impute the union of Mr. Pitt with the Earl of Shelburne. Friendship was not the base of their coalescence, and will be no impediment to their separation. Friendship, says Cicero, is a rarity amongst statesmen*. It is probable, that no great association of sentiments connects him with the Earl of Shelburne, and the friends of his father, and the friends of the constitution still trust, that he will send no busy messenger to the venerable shade of great Achilles, with the sad tale, ' that Pyrrhus is degenerate †'.

If great and good men will not support the Earl of Shelburne's administration, the very

---

* Veræ amicitiæ rarissime inveniuntur in iis, qui in honoribus, reque publica, versantur.

† —— Referres ergo hæc et nuncius ibis
Pelidæ genitori: illi mea tristia facta,
Degeneremque Neoptolemum narrare memento.   VIRG.

converse of character will answer his end just as well. The noble Lord's situation is most accommodating, and if little bad men prolong his power, he will compound for their virtues. —Let him be supported, he cares not how. The maxim reprobated by the Foxites * is the Earl of Shelburne's maxim entirely—*to retain power by any means.*—Aid is welcome to him from all quarters. He would detach no less a person than an Irish Earl to gain a news-paper to his interest; and whilst (for the sake of form) he refused an audience to one editor, he bestowed one hundred pounds upon another editor. He knew the first hated, and supposed the second might not hate him; thus he balanced the possible fidelity of the one, against the positive enmity of the other. But there is always a resource in the principles of a mean politician. Where there is no decent pride there can be no honest passion. A *hint* given in private, to the editor rejected in public, produced the effect; and, from being the most clamorous against him, he suddenly feels a zeal, like inspiration, in the Earl of Shelburne's favour. I could be more explicit upon this subject; but for confidence perhaps I have said enough; for the full fact, infinitely too

* Flectere si neques superos, Acheronta movebo.

little.

little. When Mr. Fox was secretary of state, the greater number of the news-papers were offered to him. I understand his remark was—'That he could only fear their friendship, their abuse could not fail to be of advantage to him.' All the world will allow, that their acknowledged talents and untainted probity deserved a better countenance. To this reply of Mr. Fox, and to the generous patronage of the Earl of Shelburne, the public is indebted for all the argument and wit which have lately occupied these prints, compared to the stile of which, the scurrility of Billingsgate has the refinement of St. James's. They are indeed eminent in the public esteem, and cannot fail to be material to the Earl of Shelburne. So much the more, as several of them have been these ten years past representing the noble Lord, as a public incendiary, the father of rebellion, and the enemy of the state.

But this is attributable to his art in working wonders.—It is fortunate that he was not born in an age when witchery was persecuted through godliness. The Earl of Shelburne has wrought another miracle, which yields to nothing since the days of apostolic conversion.

SIR

Sir James Lowther gives the King a ship of the line, full manned, at his own expence.

Sir, I have nothing to do with the low doubts and sordid conjectures which have been propagated upon this event. I do not mention the report either that this gift is offered upon the chance of a peace, and the ship's never being half finished—or that it is the bargain for a peerage—or that it is an act of cunning in the Earl of Shelburne; and that the money is to come from the treasury—nor to quote the poet upon Sir James,

' Now saves the *nation*, and now saves *a groat*.'

But with a view to give my contempt to the whole mass of suspicions—the character of Sir James Lowther is the amplest refutation of every charge. When I consider the virtue of his heart and the wisdom of his head: the excellence of his morals and the expansion of his mind: his honourable conduct in all his private duties: his exactness, punctuality, and rectitude in all his commercial dealings: his long life of private faith and public probity—I must take the act precisely as it appears to be, *a deed of pure and spotless patriotism.*

Such an event, two hundred years ago, might have brought fufpicions of forcery upon the Earl of Shelburne. But this is an enlightened age, and why fhould any man wonder that the Earl of Bute's fon-in-law fhould prefent the crown with fuch a gift, when Lord Shelburne and the Duke of Grafton are of the royal cabinet. The illuminations which brighten upon the world from the King's council are wonderful. His Majefty's prefent Lord Privy Seal concurs in employing the fon of Samuel Vaughan to negociate a peace for England at the Court of Verfailles.—Adieu to prejudice for evermore.

Good nature is ever confident. There are fome excellent people in this country, who have a confolation in the worft difafters. The Earl of Shelburne has bound himfelf to the meafure of a more equal reprefentation in parliament. Let him give us that, and the moft infamous adminiftration cannot injure us—Nay, if the Earl of Shelburne himfelf continue minifter he cannot hurt us. This is true wifdom, and it muft be the more admitted in this proteftant country, as it is the chief bafis of the Roman Catholic faith. The Pope is not held perfonally infallible. He is only fo at the head of a general council. It is the number

ber that constitutes the infallibility. If one or two hundred additional members are added to the present House of Commons, it will be then impossible that body can be guilty of ignorance or prostituted to any act of baseness. The House of Lords has always emerged from servitude in proportion to the accession of new peers. All the administrations of this reign have been lovers of constitutional liberty, and to secure it, his present Majesty has exceeded even James the First in ennobling his subjects. I will not say that the Earl of Shelburne may not *appear* friendly to a change in the representation, but I must rescue his character from the disgrace of being supposed amicable to that measure, in mere compliance with the spirit of a letter to the Wiltshire committee, or any declaration in the House of Lords. The noble Earl is bound by no declaration. He is above all these infirmities. I doubt not he *may* be as much a public friend, as he *will* be a private enemy to the plan of equalising the representation. He would do any thing rather than lose his station. This is not an hour to hazard an insurrection, otherwise I should credit the report of his calling in the old ministry. That he would gladly join ' *that beast, that thing**, which he could not call a man,' I can well

---

* Epithets applied to Lord North, by Lord Shelburne in the House of Peers.

imagine. But there is some consideration even for the old party. Lord North well knows, there is a wide space between misfortune and contempt, between political disgrace and moral infamy. The Lord Advocate of Scotland was *not* proscribed by Mr. Fox, and of this, the Earl of Shelburne took immediate advantage. But Mr. Dundas has yet to account to the world, why he abandoned his former party. The acknowledged infamy of his political opinions, renders him unworthy of my notice; and if his desertion from his old friends, has been unconditional to them, he is beneath the dignity of resentment. If all failed the Earl of Shelburne, I am not sure that he may not adopt those very principles which he reprobated in Mr. Fox, and which obliged the latter to quit the cabinet. I believe he would forget his own nature to please the *Commons*. He has the Lords in his *pocket*, and the King in his *hand*.

To the Sovereign he has been pretty uniform, and I dare say he would have been entirely so, if it were not necessary to the ridiculous consistency of his character, that he should contradict himself upon every public opinion he has ever delivered. The Earl of Shelburne, upon his own appointment to the treasury, maintained the doctrine of the King's unqualified power of conferring offices

fices and honours. Five months before this, upon Lord Sackville's being called to the peerage, the Earl of Shelburne questioned his Majesty's right even to create a peer, and quoted Lord Chancellor West against it. A man of the first impression would call this audacious nonsense. Merely to ennoble a man, according to the current rate of the peerage, supposes nothing of much interest to the nation. But every subject has some concern in the conduct of a minister. He has a scope for mischief, and is therefore responsible. If the King's unqualified power of making a peer be a questionable point, his power of making a minister is surely fifty times more so.

This however is a small defect in the scale of the noble Lord's conduct. He knows, that all the slaughter of the last century has originated in too free an exercise of the prerogative. Yet the noble Lord has delivered sentiments upon that subject too valuable not to have made some impression in the Royal bosom. What is it to the people, whether they are injured by the *prerogative*, or by the *influence* of the crown? A dirk wounds as fatally as a poniard. Much labour has indeed been employed at the Revolution to define the prerogative, but the Earl of Shelburne knows it still contains enough of a

fortunate

fortunate ambiguity under the maze of which every neceſſary effect of influence may be derived. The noble Lord's opinions upon *this*, upon *American independence*, upon a *king of Mahrattas*, upon *reviving the negative*, &c. have had their due weight at St. James's, and I believe he is as confident in the ſincerity of his preſent Majeſty's attachment as any of his ſervants can be.

This is a ſerious hour, important to the liberties of the nation and the dignity of the empire, beyond any period in the Britiſh annals. It is material to his Majeſty to conſult, not indeed what the world calls, the *King's friends*, but the friends of the Engliſh conſtitution, becauſe they are the true friends of the houſe of Brunſwick. Experiments have been hazarded in the early parts of his reign, which made the adminiſtrations of that time univerſally execrable, and a loving ſubject would have leſs cauſe to lament, if the infamy of his ſervants did not then impart ſome portion of injury to a character, whom the laws have generouſly lifted above the neceſſity of having any intereſt in the vicious principles and malignant artifices of his miniſters. His preſent Majeſty is bleſſed with many virtues, but muſt, in common with all the kings upon earth, wiſh

an

an increase of his own authority, and consequently a diminution of his people's privileges. The Earl of Shelburne is well understood. Even the appearance of a design to hold another struggle with the free spirit of the nation might raise a flame, which neither power nor corruption itself could extinguish. In this country, profligate as it is, there yet lingers a strong regard for liberty. A British bosom is apt to glow at the sound of it, and the splendid merit of preserving that best gift of God, which is expelled from every other kingdom in Europe, might stimulate indolence, and animate even luxury herself, to consecrate at the altar of freedom. Original excellence is the most absolute, and the virtue without example, has a double claim to applause. Civil liberty is proscribed by the rest of Europe, and millions of Britons can be levied by the bare glory of affording an asylum to this illustrious fugitive. This were an enthusiasm upon the base of reason, and enthusiasts are always the most dangerous enemies. If I am capable of forming an opinion, THIS IS THE MOST CRITICAL MOMENT OF HIS MAJESTY'S REIGN. All his skill is necessary to direct him, and if, upon consulting his wisdom, he thinks it is for his own, for his family's, and his people's interest, to employ a minister, whose character is, in a few words, *That he is suspected by every man in the nation, who does not despise or detest him.* I have only to say in the gentle language of legal mercy, ' *God send him a good deliverance.*'

And now, Sir, without making any apology for addressing myself to you, I shall conclude this letter (in which, if I have imputed a principle to, or related an incident of, the Earl of Shelburne, which, in a single instance, shall be proved untrue, or unwarranted by his conduct and public declarations, I desire to lose all credit with the public for every other part)—I will not praise you, for if I were a panegyrist you are above my praise. The object of Sir George Savile's life has been the good of the state to which he belongs; and if the principles of this letter tend to the benefit of the Commonwealth, his sanction is without doubt secured to it. The measure is justified in the motive.

POST-

POSTSCRIPT,

TO THE RIGHT HONORABLE

JOHN Earl of STAIR.

My Lord,

I HAVE read your pamphlet with great attention. The preceding sheets will, I think, afford you intelligence upon some points which you allude to, and upon which you are certainly (or appear to be) misinformed. This postscript will delay the publication of my letter to Sir George Saville for a few hours. I have not time to make many remarks upon your performance, and in the little I shall say, the remotest disrespect is not meant to your Lordship. Your industry deserves commendation, your family is antient and honorable; the name of *Stair* is illustrious, and your own personal character is respectable.

If your pamphlet discovered principles so unquestionable, as to leave me no proper office, but that of a critic, for your sake, I should not comment upon the style of your writing. The substance of it, my Lord, is my object, and indeed you have afforded me in the first place,

L the

the ſtrongeſt *preſumptions* that you have deſerted that ſyſtem of politics which was traceable in your former publications: and in the ſecond, the ſtrongeſt *proofs* that you are inconſiſtent with yourſelf, and palpably unjuſt to others. I have but a few hours to ſhew that you have done this, and I thank you for rendering the taſk perfectly eaſy. A review of your former profeſſed and preſent implied principles is all that is requiſite. Argument is unneceſſary. My Lord, is it fair to make no diſtinctions between the miſconduct of the Earl of Shelburne, and the open diſintereſted acts of thoſe who united with him in the month of March, and quitted him in the month of July? You could not treat of the adminiſtration of this country for the laſt nine months, without adverting to *his* bad deeds. Such a partiality would be too palpable, and the friend were fatal who ſhould ſay he was guiltleſs. You talk of a diviſion of ſpoils after the capture of St. James's. Pray, my Lord, need you be told, that except ' a lean baronetage' (to adopt your own words) a ſtar or a ſtring, no friend of Mr. Fox's has any thing to boaſt from his adminiſtration. The Earl of Shelburne knew that honours without emoluments were of little real value, and enriched his own friends. Malice, until this moment,

has

has not dared to advance so bold a falsehood, as that Mr. Fox, or his friends, sought the ends of avarice, in preference to the public good.

I do not mean, my Lord, to question the correctness of your calculations, as to public debt, and public credit. If you are right, the facts you publish are dreadful. So great is the national debt, that the state must pay fifteen millions annually, and the revenue cannot be made to exceed twelve millions. The state cannot now pay more in interest, than at the rate of thirteen shillings and six pence to the pound—If the war continues another year, the abilities of the nation will not pay more than twelve shillings and a penny. And you despair of one pound of the principal being discharged at all. This is the abridged import of your calculations and deductions, and it is a most deplorable review of the condition of this unhappy country. In your pamphlet of last January you declare, that these unexampled calamities were brought upon this nation by the ministers of that time. No language could be more clear than that in which you conveyed your execration of them, and of the accursed war in which they plunged this country. How am I to account, my Lord, for your panegyrics upon these very ministers, in your present publication, and for conveying something more than a mere implication, that it would be for the common interest if they were restored? In your former pamphlet you asserted, that the ministers would ruin the nation. In the present, you affirm that the nation is ruined. From page 17 to 18 is engrossed with proving the state has no resources; and in page 2, you applaud the former ministers *for not despairing of resources.* You declare you cannot tell ' on what fair ground of honest candor they were dispossessed'—You could give fifty reasons yourself about a year ago for dispossessing them—No man ever condemned them in terms more unequivocal. You say, in page 3, the new ministry had neither the *will* nor the *power* to change the system—My Lord, why would you be so careless in assertions? they proved that they had both will and power, and did very materially change the system. Was the relinquishment of the American war no change of system? Was the peace of Ireland, and getting 20,000 seamen, no change of system? Were the contractors bill, the revenue officers bill, the civil list bill, no change of system? The administration lasted just three months, and in that time this important change of system took place. If you do not think this a change of system, I

believe

believe, my Lord, you are the only man in the kingdom who does not.

You affect to ridicule the acclamations of the nation upon the change in March, and addresses, you say, page 40, 'flowed in from every quarter.'——I do not remember that a single address came from Scotland; but certainly the court was crowded with addresses from every part of England and Ireland upon the occasion. Will you allow any thing, my Lord, for the sense of mankind? Do you think there was ever a measure, in which the hearts and the judgements of the people more sincerely concurred than in that change? Then wherefore the general mistrust of England—the universal discontent of Ireland? I'll tell you, my Lord, because that administration no longer exists. I am sorry to say, my Lord, that in page 37 you lose sight of liberality as well as justice; no lover of civil liberty can with an honest motive sneer at the Irish volunteers. I speak with deference when I presume you are not conversant in Irish politics. You was at the election of Lord Lauderdale: if you disapprove the conduct of the Irish, you had an opportunity of replying to Lord Hopetoun, who pronounced a most flattering eulogium upon the volunteers. Be assured, my my Lord, he will derive more honour from it, than your Lordship will receive from that peculiar ſtyle of flattery to Lord Shelburne in the ſame paragraph of your pamphlet, that ſneers at the Iriſh. You are friendly to Lord Shelburne, I think I need not entertain one doubt of it. For your information, my Lord (though I believe not for your Lordſhip's conſolation) I will let you know the truth. The Iriſh are ſolidly diſcontented. They have no confidence in this adminiſtration, and it is only the remoteneſs of your reſidence which could make you ignorant of that man's name, who of all the men upon earth is moſt deteſted in the kingdom of Ireland. But how ſtands Mr. Fox, you will ſay? I will tell you a public fact, my Lord, which from your ideas of Iriſh affairs, I muſt ſuppoſe, has never reached you. Mr. Montgomery, the member for Donegall (a gentleman who, to the great grief of his friends, reſts under a general ſuſpicion for correctneſs of intellect) made a motion in the Iriſh Parliament, diſreſpectful to Mr. Fox, and in the whole houſe not a ſingle man could be found to ſecond a motion, ridiculous in itſelf, and execrated as to its tendency. Form your own concluſion from this fact.

Upon the subject of reforms, my Lord, it gives me pain to say, you hold no measure. In page 29 you say, that ministers deserve contempt for boasting, that œconomy would produce much good, and in the very next page you say, it will be grateful and advantageous to the public. In page 33 again you say, the public gratitude and thanks are due for the considerable reformations already begun, and in the next page to this you attempt in a very particular manner to disparage the chief reformer; and, lest your own good prose should fail, you call in Shakespeare's poetry to your assistance. This may seem strange to some people: it is no matter of surprize to me. You abused the ministry of Lord North in January; in November you defend it. Even upon this subject you would shelter him from censure. You say, ministers scarce ever have an influence sufficient to eradicate abuses. I am sure, my Lord, very few men in the nation will agree with you, that Lord North, for one minister, had not influence enough to check the shameful abuses in public offices. Every good man in this country seems agreed, that Mr. Burke in his conduct as paymaster was more than barely consistent: he is said to have acted disinterestedly even to a degree that was noble. And yet you are more sore upon that point than all the rest.

Do you think it was criminal to make his son deputy paymaſter, at a ſalary of 1000 pounds a year, which place is ſaid to have produced 12000 pounds annually to his predeceſſor Mr. Caſwell? Or are you diſpleaſed, that, inſtead of making fifty thouſand pounds a year, like his predeceſſor, Mr. Burke ſhould reduce his own profits to four thouſand pounds a year? Do I overſtate the produce of Mr. Rigby? Has your Lordſhip read the reports of the commiſſioners of accounts? Seriouſly then, my Lord, do you think any man will value your heart the more for the contents of page 34? I believe it cannot injure the reputation of your head.

Let us oppoſe your theory to Mr. Burke's practice. You had the full ſcope of imagination; yet all the retrenchment *you* could recommend was to deprive the commanders of regiments of the profits of cloathing, page 25. The next moment you ſay, this is *no* object for retrenchment, for it does not pay the expence of attending the regiments, and then again conclude with remarking, that it is the moſt ſtriking object of reformation, and from which only an increaſe of revenue could be expected.

Military ideas were natural to an Earl of Stair, but I think the Colonels will not much thank

thank you for your attachment to the military; you are now a soldier, then a financier, and at another time a commiſſary. Sometimes for the army, ſometimes for the public, and ſometimes for neither. Your Lordſhip is wondrouſly enamoured of the old miniſtry. In January you called the American war the moſt accurſed this country ever waged; in November you ſay ‘ the late miniſters deſerved well of the public for the great and unparalleled attention with which they ſupported the American war.’ You follow this with a comment which Lord Germaine might well have dictated, and the paſſage is concluded with a compliment to the Admiralty, as warm as my Lord Mulgrave himſelf could have expreſſed it. The wonder is, my Lord, how all this can come from *you*. I underſtand, you ſeldom approved the political proceedings of the corporation of Edinburgh, and yet your paragraph, in favour of that miniſtry whom you execrated in January, is almoſt literally in the ſhape of one of the reſolutions of that Edinburgh meeting, which would *not* return thanks to the King for changing the miniſtry.

But you make amends for all by your opinion upon the ſubject of the peace. You ſaid laſt January, that ‘ no peace ſhort of abſolute ruin

ruin could be pronounced a bad one;' in November you urge the neceſſity of peace, in p. 3. in p. 28 you ſay it is the only œconomy; and then you add what would open your character ſufficiently to me, if in p. 35 you did not diſcover yourſelf as clearly as noon-day. In that paſſage all your inconſiſtency is accounted for. The Earl of Stair adopts not merely the ſentiments, but the very words of the Earl of Shelburne and of Lord North. If we cannot get peace upon our terms, let us carry on the war with our lives and fortunes. Had the firſt lord of the treaſury been at your elbow, I could not wiſh to ſee a paſſage hit off more completely to his purpoſe. Has the Earl of Shelburne, my Lord, given you any reaſons to think, that Lord Rockingham under-rated your talents? or is it your object, firſt to convince him that you think ſo, that he may afterwards give a ſanction to your ſelf-love?

But, my Lord, in page 40 there is an aſſertion which I can hardly pardon. In matters of opinion great latitude is allowable; in points of fact there is no alternative. You ſay that a conteſt for power firſt diſcovers a difference of opinion in matters of public import, evidently alluding to Lord Shelburne's appointment to the treaſury. My Lord, I am aſtoniſhed you can be

ignorant

ignorant that the matter of Mr. Fox's refignation had been completely cleared up, the laft day of the laft feffions, in the Houfe of Lords, to the fatisfaction of the whole nation. *The Earl of Shelburne convicted himself of falfehood.* I will not fuppofe, at leaft I will not affert, that you are acquainted with this circumftance. The paffage as it ftands, were this fact within your knowledge, would greatly difhonour your Lordfhip's character.

I entirely agree with you, my Lord, ' that a man would gain more credit, and certainly would be much more fure of preferment, by an ingenious rhetorical apology for the want of every human virtue, than by poffeffing, without the power of announcing them, every great and good quality that can adorn human nature.' This I think, my Lord, was precifely the qualification that recommended your good countryman Mr. Dundas, to the Earl of Shelburne. Men of that defcription are always welcome to him.

It very well becomes you, my Lord, after alluding to the Lord Advocate of Scotland, to attempt to be merry upon orators. The jeft was well-timed, if it were fuccefsful. You do not hold a *certain clafs* of fpeakers in greater contempt

contempt than I do; but you do not seem disposed to distinguish, and there we differ. Your story of the pea-shooter answers no end that I can see, but to shew how little the Earl of Stair values one of the noblest of intellectual arts. I give your Lordship credit for the elegance of your taste; but if you expected this passage would promote the reputation of your wit, I fear you have greatly deceived yourself.

Every sensible reader of your present work will be surprized to find a desertion of your professed principles. It cannot fail to be a matter of astonishment that the same man, who in January reprobates the Tories for losing America, should in November imply a manifest wish that these very Tories were restored to conduct the government. To me, my Lord, it appears in a different light. I have formed an opinion of your Lordship from some parts of your former pamphlet, which makes your present work the less inconsistent. In that you did assert some mistakes, which any shopkeeper could set you right in. You said (for some strange purpose) that the greatest æra of England's felicity, was from 1765 to 1775, and that imagination can scarcely surpass it. My Lord, I affirm, that this country, since the massacres of the last century, never felt so

much

much domestic distress and foreign disgrace, as in these very ten years. Do you forget, my Lord, that it was in this very interval, the constitution was stabbed in the affair of the Middlesex election—That the despotic attempt was made to cut up liberty by the roots, by general warrants—that the greatest and wisest men in this country affirmed openly in both Houses of Parliament, that the people's representatives were traitors, and sold the rights of the nation—That the crown was assailed with clamours from all parts of the kingdom—that the soldiery was let loose and assumed the office of the magistracy—and that the whole nation fell into an uproar, superior to any interior distraction since the civil wars. This proves our domestic felicity in that period. For exterior glory, look to the contemptible business of Corsica, the shameful affair of Falkland's Island. The loss of the Swedish liberties without a single effort to secure them. (Indeed *this* is easily accounted for—The cause of the King and ministry of Sweden was the cause of the King and ministry of England.)—It was in this period, his Majesty assured his Parliament from year to year, that he was making efforts to effect a peace between Russia and the Porte. The people of this country naturally expected their Sovereign would have

have had the glory of making this peace; when, to their difappointment, and to his difgrace, the French ambaſſador at Conſtantinople ſnatched away this honour, and ratified the peace of the North, before a ſyllable of it was known in this country. Good effects, my Lord, flowed from this. They are manifeſt, and the Empreſs was certainly as ſincere in her mediation between us and Holland laſt April, as your Lordſhip was in your political principles laſt January.

But, my Lord, you went farther ſtill in your former pamphlet. Deſtitute of any apparent object but that of injuring yourſelf, you talked in high terms of the advantages of the peace of Paris. From that moment I fuſpected you. The diſhonour which this nation has ſuſtained in that event are acknowledged by all Europe, and can only be defended by the adherents of certain ſtateſmen. I have in theſe ſheets cautiouſly avoided falling into national reflections. They are too common in this country; and indeed it is difficult in treating of the politics of the preſent reign, to eſcape this general malady. Diſtinctly from political prejudice I have for Scotland the greateſt reſpect—for Scotchmen the greateſt affection. To taint them would be to wound myſelf. My ſociety is in

a great

a great part compofed of the natives of that country, and I do not dread that I fhall ever lament the connection. You extort the neceffity of faying, that you could not in thefe glaring inftances deviate from public facts, unlefs with a view to cover the guilt of Lord Bute and his minions. In your prefent work the fame motive meets me in every page (except indeed in your calculations). To ferve Lord Shelburne is in effect to ferve Lord Bute: he is a branch of the old trunk, and it was only a blaft of an ill wind that broke him off. Public fhame might prevent Lord North from joining him now, but in the GREAT END, you all agree. It will be wrong to fay, that the Earl of Shelburne quitted the miniftry in 1768, becaufe he would not fupport the prevailing fyftem. The Earl of Shelburne put the feal of State to what the Duke de Choifeul affirmed to be, and afterwards proved to be, a falfehood, and he was forced out in confequence. The truth is, even that adminiftration were afraid to confide to him the real intentions of government. There is a faying recorded of a man who knew him well; he faid, he had known men who *became* Jefuits, but the only man he ever heard of who was *born* a Jefuit, was the Earl of Shelburne. Malagrida, my Lord, was not to be trufted at any time. I will not difhonour you by faying,

you

you are the *direct* advocate of this minister. It is the greatest injury I can do an honest man. Perhaps it would suit your peculiar turn to say, you are the friend of no party. Be it so, my Lord; but I always suspect this appearance of implicit neutrality. It is seldom solid. You love to quote Shakespeare, and I will conclude this postscript with a passage from that celebrated author, leaving your Lordship to make the application.

⸺⸺This is some fellow,
Who, having been praised for bluntness, doth affect
A saucy boldness, and constrains the garb
Quite from his nature. He can't flatter, he⸺
An honest mind and plain, he must speak truth;
And they will take it, so; if not, he's plain.
These kind of knaves I know, which in this plainness
Harbour more craft, and more corrupter ends,
Than twenty silly ducking observants
That stretch their duties nicely.

I have the honour to be,

MY LORD, &c.

www.ingramcontent.com/pod-product-compliance
Lightning Source LLC
Chambersburg PA
CBHW020900160426
43192CB00007B/1010